Porcupines

by **Judith Jango-Cohen**

Marshall Cavendish
Benchmark
New York

For Ariana Panetta, with love

The author thanks Doug Sanders, editor, for his perceptive eye.

Series consultant
James G. Doherty
General Curator, Bronx Zoo, New York

Marshall Cavendish Benchmark
99 White Plains Road
Tarrytown, NY 10591-9001
www.marshallcavendish.us

Library of Congress Cataloging-in-Publication Data

Jango-Cohen, Judith.
Porcupines / by Judith Jango-Cohen.— 1st ed.
p. cm. — (Animals, animals)
Summary: "Describes the physical characteristics, behavior, and habitat of porcupines"—Provided by publisher.
Includes bibliographical references and index.
ISBN 0–7614–1868–7
1. Porcupines—Juvenile literature. I. Title. II. Series.

QL737.R652J25 2005
599.35'97—dc22
2004021443

Photo research by Joan Meisel

Cover photo: S.J. Krasemann/Peter Arnold, Inc.

Series redesign by Adam Mietlowski

Printed in China

1 3 5 6 4 2

Contents

1 Introducing Porcupines   5

2 Gnawing and Napping   13

3 Prickly Protection   21

4 Cycle of Life   29

5 Porcupines and People   37

Glossary   44

Find Out More   46

Index   48

 1 Introducing Porcupines

A South African porcupine and her small *porcupette* waddle down a dry riverbed. Up ahead, a young lion crouches, silently waiting. As the porcupines draw near, the lion pounces. Instantly, the porcupines spin around, pointing their bristly backs and tails toward the hunter. They raise their manes of wiry hair and flare their prickly quills. Thrashing their tails, they shake their hollow "rattle quills." These special quills sound a warning to *predators*. The lion inches one paw toward the porcupette, trying to flip it over. But the mother porcupine lunges at the lion, tail-first. Surprised, the young lion roars and leaps away from the spiky weapon. A lion is armed with slashing claws

A young lion is not sure how to attack this young South African porcupine.

Porcupines are found on five of the seven continents.

and powerful jaws. But these weapons do not ensure a victory. Porcupine quills often pierce and kill predators such as leopards, pythons, mountain lions, eagles, and weasels.

Porcupines live on every continent except Antarctica and Australia. Scientists divide the twenty-three *species*, or kinds, of porcupines into two families. One family is the Old World porcupines. They live in Africa, Asia, and Europe. Old World porcupines are ground-dwelling animals that eat mostly roots and fallen fruit. New World porcupines are found in North America and South America. These porcupines can climb trees to feed on leaves, nuts, fruits, and bark.

The North American porcupine survives in a range of *climates*, from snowy Alaska to sunny northern Mexico. It is the only porcupine species found in Canada and the United States. North American porcupines have long guard hairs to help protect them from rain and snow. To shield themselves from the cold, these porcupines grow a thick layer of fur. They shed this fur each spring.

The North American porcupine is not often seen by people. Like all porcupines, it is *nocturnal*, active mostly at night. It is sometimes hidden while nibbling in the leafy limbs of trees.

New World porcupines also include the *prehensile-tailed* porcupines of Mexico, Central America, and South America. These porcupines rarely come down from the rain-forest trees. Their muscular, prehensile tails wind snugly around branches. Used as climbing tools, their tails have no quills. Hanging upside down, these acrobats can gather fruit and seeds from the tips of tree limbs. Up in the treetops they avoid hunters that live on the forest floor. If cornered on the ground, a prehensile-tailed porcupine may growl, stamp its hind feet, bite, or curl into a prickly ball.

Species Chart

A full-grown South African porcupine may weigh as much as 66 pounds (30 kilograms).

Prehensile-tailed porcupines may weigh up to 11 pounds (5 kilograms).

A male North American porcupine weighs about 14 pounds (6.4 kilograms). Females weigh about 3 pounds (1.4 kilograms) less.

The South African porcupine, an Old World species, cannot climb trees. But its coat of quills provides plenty of protection from roving predators. Some quills can be as long as 16 inches (40 centimeters). That is four times the length of a North American porcupine's quills.

Besides these lance-like quills, South African porcupines have two other types of quills. They have quills with jagged sawtooth edges. They also grow "rattle quills" on their tails. Rattle quills form first as pointy-tipped tail quills. But as they grow the tip snaps off and the spongy material inside falls out. A hollow, open-tipped quill is left. When the quills brush against the bristly hairs on the porcupine's tail, they make a hissing sound.

Both Old World and New World porcupines belong to a group of animals called *rodents.* There are about 1,700 rodent species, including squirrels, chipmunks, prairie dogs, gophers, mice, muskrats, gerbils, hamsters, and guinea pigs. Beavers are the largest rodents in North America, followed by porcupines.

The word *rodent* comes from the Latin *rodere* meaning "to *gnaw.*" Four front teeth, called *incisors,* allow rodents to bite on bark or nibble on nuts. Gnawing wears a rodent's incisors down, but these teeth grow continuously, lasting a lifetime.

Relatives of the porcupine, beavers are North America's largest rodents.

2 Gnawing and Napping

The sun slides over New York's Catskill Mountains on a cold December morning. Pine needles sparkle with a sprinkling of snow. On the forest floor, fallen leaves are covered with a clean, frosty coat. The woods are still, except for the screeching coming from a pile of rocks. Two rows of footprints lead into an opening between the stones. Inside two porcupines—the one occupant and an intruder—have come face to face.

North American porcupines usually do not share a *den*. When dens are in short supply, quarrels may occur. Since North American porcupines are unable to dig their own homes, they search for empty shelters. Cozy crannies in rock piles are the most popular

Prehensile-tailed porcupines make their dens in trees or in hollow logs.

13

winter hideaways. Porcupines also use hollow tree trunks, holes in rotting logs, abandoned badger and coyote dens, and barns.

The North American porcupine does not sleep in its den year round like raccoons and beavers. Most of the time a porcupine will sleep out on a tree limb, with its legs dangling down. In the spring, it may hole up in a den to escape biting flies or pelting rain. In hot *habitats,* porcupines retreat into cool burrows

A North American porcupine has found a sunny spot for a nap.

North American porcupines often station themselves in trees during winter storms.

when the heat becomes extreme. In regions with cold winters, porcupines nestle into shelters once temperatures fall below freezing. Their stubby legs make it tough to travel in deep snow, so North American porcupines choose dens close to a food source.

During the winter, porcupines nibble on evergreen needles and tree bark. They remember their favorite trees and return to them each year. Scars from the previous year's feeding block the flow of sap inside the trunk. The sticky sap that builds up above the scar offers a sweet meal.

The Porcupine:

As shown by the shape of its jaws and teeth . . .

Inside and Out

. . . a porcupine is well designed for gnawing on the bark of trees.

A porcupine uses its teeth to shave off the often tough outer layer of bark.

Porcupines tear into bark with their long incisors. These sharp teeth are made stronger by an outer layer of orange *enamel.* Porcupines peel and eat the thin bark of limbs and young tree trunks. But they dislike thick, crusty bark, so they chip away at it until they reach the smooth, inner wood. Hooking their top incisors into the tree, they shave off slivers with their lower incisors. Their sturdy back *molars* then chop and mash the wood.

Porcupines usually lose weight in the winter, eating only bark and evergreen needles. Fortunately spring brings tender buds and blossoms. In summer, porcupines feast on dandelions, buttercups, and bluebells. Apples, acorns, and seeds provide *nutrients* in the fall.

Porcupines must stay alert for predators, especially when they are feeding on the ground. A porcupine's eyesight is poor. But its hearing is good, and it can rely on its keen sense of smell. Porcupines are not easy targets for most predators. However, there is one hunter that has a knack for turning porcupines into a snack.

Did You Know . . .

Although North American porcupines are at home in trees, they often tumble out of them. A scientist studying thirty-seven porcupine skeletons discovered that thirteen showed signs of broken bones.

Prickly Protection

With its hair and quills raised in alarm, a porcupine turns its bristling backside toward a hungry fisher. The long-tailed fisher, which looks like a fluffy weasel, leaps over the porcupine's back. For a moment, the fisher and its *prey* are face to face. But the porcupine reels around tail-first, hiding its face with its feet. Again, the clever fisher springs over the porcupine, continuing the assault. Soon the porcupine starts to wobble and sway, and its tail begins to droop.

Fishers hunt their prickly prey by trying to make them tired and dizzy. Then they can slip a paw under the porcupine and flip it over. This exposes the porcupine's underbelly, which is free of quills.

Fishers have a varied diet that includes chipmunks, shrews, snowshoe hares, and porcupines.

Fishers also kill porcupines by darting at their faces. They try to bite the porcupine before their prey can swat them with its tail. Despite their skillful hunting, fishers are sometimes killed by quills.

Porcupine quills are a special kind of thick, stiff hair. Like hair, quills grow and are then shed. Fully grown quills shrink at the base until they loosen and fall out. New quills then grow in to replace them.

North American porcupines have scale-like *barbs* on the tips of their quills. You can feel the barbs with your fingers, but they are visible only with a microscope. Barbs allow the quill to glide point-first into a predator's flesh. But a tug on the base of the quill causes the barbs to flare out like open umbrellas. This makes removing the quills a difficult and painful job.

Usually quills lie flat, tucked in among a porcupine's long hairs. But when a porcupine is disturbed or becomes alarmed, muscles raise the quills. If an animal comes into contact with the prickly quills, they stick into its flesh. When the animal pulls away, the quills detach from the porcupine and remain in the victim.

For a curious dog, coming into contact with a porcupine can have sharp
and painful results.

When threatened, porcupines present their bristling backsides.

Did You Know . . .

How many quills are in the coat of a North American porcupine? A scientist once tried to count the quills on a dead porcupine. He got as far as 1,900 and gave up. Based on his count, he guessed that there are about 30,000.

Being pierced by quills is not only painful, it can also cause serious wounds or even death. A face full of quills can prevent an animal from eating or seeing clearly. Quills can also work their way into an animal and cut its insides.

The lightest touch to its body will cause a porcupine to swiftly raise its quills.

Porcupines are master climbers that have learned the art of blending in.

Porcupines attack only as a last resort. First they try to scare away predators. When threatened, porcupines' bodies begin to tremble, causing their front and back teeth to clack and clatter. They also release a foul odor from an opening above the base of their tails. But if these warnings do not work, the porcupine can always turn to its quills.

Quills protect a porcupine against predators. But during the mating season, competing male porcupines may turn these sharp weapons on one another.

Did You Know . . .

While trying to capture a porcupine, a scientist was smacked by the animal's prickly tail. The porcupine's slap left a patch of quills piercing his skin. The scientist was able to remove all of the quills except one, which had burrowed into his upper arm. The quill traveled to his lower arm, where it poked out two days later.

4 Cycle of Life

A blizzard of white quills blankets the base of an oak tree. Some quills lie in piles. Others poke from leaves and twigs like thorns. The forest floor is torn up, and tufts of hair are scattered around.

On a branch, directly above this battleground, are two male porcupines. The victor leans against the trunk, two quills poking from its nose. The other porcupine crouches at the far end of the limb. The cause of the conflict, a female, sits in a nearby tree.

Fall is mating season for North American porcupines. Males battle one another using their sharp incisors and thrashing tails. The winning male chases off his rivals and stays with the female until

This young crested porcupine knows to stick close to its mother for protection.

she is ready to mate with him. After mating, males and females separate until the following fall.

Seven months after mating, the female porcupine gives birth to a single porcupette. The abundant spring plants provide nutrients for the mother. Like every female *mammal,* a mother porcupine produces milk for her young. While the baby drinks, mother and young often "sing" together. The mother's low mewing blends with the baby's high cooing to form a soothing duet.

North American porcupettes drink their mother's milk for about four months.

Crested porcupines give birth to a litter of one to three porcupettes.

Newborn porcupines have eight teeth—four back teeth and four front incisors. The incisors look like little white pegs. They do not yet have the orange enamel coating.

A porcupette is born fully armored with quills. The quills are soft at first, but they stiffen within an hour. Unlike adults, with both white and black quills, a newborn's quills are all black, like its hair. A porcupette *instinctively* knows how to use its quills. If disturbed, it bristles its quills and smacks its tail without having learned these behaviors from its mother.

For the first six weeks after giving birth, mothers limit their usual wandering in search of food. They stay near their young, which are not yet strong enough to travel far. During the day, the mother sleeps on a tree limb. The baby cannot climb the tree, so it stays at the bottom. It naps in small nooks under logs and rocks or in a hollow at the base of the tree. In the evening, the mother moves about the treetops finding food. The baby stays nearby on the ground. Its black quills and hair help it blend in with the shadowy woods.

From her high perch, a mother porcupine can spot the best places to feed.

Though good climbers, porcupines have been known to tumble out of trees. Growing babies practice their climbing skills, scurrying up trunks and crawling along branches.

34

Gradually, the porcupette learns how to climb, and it joins its mother. Curved claws on its front and hind paws latch onto the tree trunk. They also hook into tight nooks in the bark. On the bottom of each paw is a hairless, rubbery pad that grips the tree. While a porcupine climbs, stiff bristles on the underside of its tail dig into the bark. They prevent the porcupine from sliding back down.

Young porcupines must learn not only how to climb trees but also how to get down. Porcupines descend from a tree tail-first, using their tails to feel their way down. Once they have mastered climbing, young porcupines are ready for a life of gnawing and napping.

Porcupines and People

About midnight, two campers lie awake. They are listening as a whimpering creature gets ever closer to their tent. The animal waddles up the side of their tent but quickly slips down. Then the creature shuffles to the front of the tent and gnaws the hikers' sweaty boots. The campers soon discover that porcupines are common nighttime visitors.

Today people who discover a North American porcupine are usually intrigued and amused. But in the past the porcupine was viewed as an important source of food. During the winter, porcupine meat became vital for the survival of Native Americans. They so respected the porcupine that they did not allow their dogs to gnaw on its bones. They burned the bones or

Some people consider porcupines to be pests because they gnaw on the wooden walls of cabins and sheds.

threw them into the river. In the 1600s and 1700s, European settlers relied on porcupine meat as well.

People rarely eat North American porcupines today. But porcupines often eat things that belong to people, such as backpacks, boots, wooden tools, and canoe paddles. Why? The porcupines are seeking a needed supply of sodium. Sodium helps muscles and nerves work properly. Since sodium is found in sweat, sweat-soaked items attract porcupines. Plywood also contains sodium, so porcupines gnaw on signs, out-houses, and sheds made of this material.

Of course backpacks and sheds are just snacks for porcupines. Their main meals come from trees. Porcupines' taste for trees has caused conflicts between porcupines and people. Timber companies do not like porcupines nibbling away at their profits.

In the 1900s, porcupines began increasing in number. Their population grew so large that people started poisoning them. Some states paid hunters to shoot them. Without knowing it though, people had helped the porcupine population to grow by trapping predators, such as fishers, for their fur.

Did You Know . . .

Native Americans valued the porcupine not only as food. Hollowed-out quills poked into maple trees collected the dripping, sweet sap. The tail, with its sturdy bristles, provided a hair brush. Quills, dyed with plant pigments, decorated belts, boxes, bracelets, and moccasins.

This Native American, of the Lakota Sioux tribe, is wearing a traditional porcupine headdress.

A porcupine balances on some branches while nibbling its leafy lunch.

Governments no longer pay people to hunt porcupines. Instead, some are releasing fishers into the wild to balance and control porcupine populations. People have also come to realize that porcupines do not cause a large loss of timber. Tree bark is eaten mostly in the winter from the trees near porcupine dens. Dens are usually in steep, rocky regions, where trees are often too difficult to log.

Porcupines do less harm to a forest than is often supposed.

As people learn more about the porcupine, they view it with new respect. They see the beneficial role porcupines play in their habitat. Porcupines feed mostly on common tree species, giving rarer trees a chance to grow. By nibbling on treetop leaves, they bring more sunlight to the forest floor. Small plants can then take root and provide shelter and food for other animals.

Scientists still have much to learn about these shy animals.

Porcupines also nip off branches and drop them to the ground. Deer and rabbits feast on these leftovers in winter. Mice and chipmunks also benefit by feeding on dropped apples that porcupines leave behind.

Scientists who study the porcupine have come to admire this quiet creature. It may be pokey, it may not see well, and it sometimes falls out of trees, but the porcupine stands up to pythons and leopards, the most fearsome of predators.

Glossary

barb: A sharp point.

climate: A region's weather conditions such as temperature, rainfall, and winds.

den: A sheltered place used to rest, hide, or sleep.

enamel: The hard, glossy coating on teeth.

gnaw: To wear away by biting or chewing.

habitat: The place where an animal lives, including the living and nonliving things in the environment.

incisors: Front teeth used for cutting.

instinctively: Acting with inborn knowledge.

mammal: A warm-blooded animal that has a backbone, fur or hair, gives birth to live young, and makes milk to feed its young.

molars: Broad, back teeth used for grinding food.

nocturnal: Active at night.

nutrients: Substances in food that provide energy and help living things to grow.

porcupette: A young porcupine.

predator: An animal that hunts and eats other animals.

prehensile: Flexible, muscular, and able to grab and hold onto something.

prey: An animal that is hunted and eaten by other animals.

rodents: Gnawing mammals such as porcupines, mice, and beavers.

species: A particular type of living thing, all of which have similar characteristics and produce similar young.

Find Out More

Books

Buxton, Ralph. *Nature's Pincushion: The Porcupine.* San Carlos, CA: Golden Gate Junior Books, 1972.

Carrick, Carol. *Ben and the Porcupine.* New York: Houghton Mifflin-Clarion Books, 1981.

Dingwall, Laima. *Porcupines.* Danbury, CT: Grolier, 1986.

Green, Carl R. *The Porcupine.* Mankato, MN: Crestwood House, 1985.

Murray, Peter. *Porcupines.* Mankato, MN: Child's World, 1993.

Schlein, Miriam. *Lucky Porcupine!* New York: Four Winds Press, 1980.

Sherrow, Victoria. *The Porcupine.* Minneapolis, MN: Dillon Press, 1991.

Swanson, Diane. *Porcupines.* Milwaukee, WI: Gareth Stevens Publishing, 2002.

Thompson-Hoffman, Susan. *Little Porcupine's Winter Den.* Norwalk, CT: Soundprints, 1992.

Web Sites

Ladywildlife's African Porcupine Page
http://ladywildlife.com/animal/africanporcupine.html

NatureWorks: Common Porcupine
http://www.nhptv.org/natureworks/porcupine.htm

Prehensile-Tailed Porcupine
http://www.americazoo.com/goto/index/mammals/207.htm

Porcupine by Chuck Fergus
http://www.pgc.state.pa.us/pgc/lib/pgc/wildlife/notes/pdf/porcupine.pdf

What about Porcupines?
http://www.pnl.gov/pals/resource_cards/porcupines.stm

Wisconsin's Prickly Rodent by Alan D. Martin
http://www.wnrmag.com/stories/1996/feb96/rodent.htm

Index

Page numbers for illustrations are in **boldface**.

map
   range, 6

beaver, 10, **11**, 14
bones, 19, 37-38

claws, **32**, 34

den, 13-14, 40
diet, 6, 15, 19

fisher, **20**, 21-22, 38
food, 6, 15, 19, 32

guard hairs, 7

mammal, 30
mating, 27, 29-30

Native Americans, 37-38, **39**
nutrients, 19, 30

paw, 35
porcupette, 5, **28**, 30, **30**, 31, **31**, 32, **34**, 35
porcupine,
   crested, **28**, **31**
   New World, 6, 7
   North American, 7, **9**, 10, 13, **14**, 15, **15**, 19, 22, 29, **30**
   Old World, 6, 10
   and people, 37-38, 40
   prehensile-tailed, 7, **9**, **12**
   South African, **4**, 5, **8**, 10
predator, **4**, 5, 6, 10, 19, **20**, 21-22, 27, 43

quills, 5, 6, 7, 10, 21, 22, **23**, 24, **24**, **25**, 27, 29, 31, 38

rattle quills, 5, 10

rodents, 10

seasons, 14-15, **15**, 19, 37, 40
senses, 19
skeleton, **16**, 19
sodium, 38

tail, 5, 7, 10, 21, 27, 31, 35
teeth, 10, 27, 31
   enamel, 19, 31
   incisors, 10, 19, 31
   molars, 19
trees, 7, 10, 14, 15, 19, 29, 32, 35, 38, 40, 41
   bark, 6, 10, 15, 19, 40

About the Author

Judith Jango-Cohen's intimate knowledge of nature comes from years of observing and photographing plants and wildlife in forests, deserts, canyons, and along seacoasts. Her thirty-four children's books reflect these experiences. They have been listed in Best Books for Children, recommended by the National Science Teacher's Association, and chosen for the Children's Literature Choice List. You can find photos from her many trips at www.agpix.com/cohen.